GROUND & CENTRE

ALSO BY KATHERINE GENET

The Wilde Grove Series

The Gathering

The Belonging

The Rising

The Singing

Wilde Grove Series 2

Follow The Wind

The Otherworld

Golden Heart

Wilde Grove Prayer Books

Prayers Of The Wildwood

Prayers Of The Beacons

Wilde Grove Bonus Stories

Becoming Morghan

The Threading

Non-Fiction

Ground & Centre

The Dreamer's Way

GROUND & CENTRE

HOW TO GROUND, CENTRE, & SHIELD YOUR ENERGY

KATHERINE GENET

WYCH ELM BOOKS

Wych Elm Books

Otago, NZ

www.wychelmbooks.com

contact@wychelmbooks.com

ISBN: 978-0-473-54506-2 (ePub) 978-0-473-54507-9 (Kindle) 978-0-473-54505-(Softcover)

CONTENTS

Being in your breath   57

INTRODUCTION

I have had a life-long interest in the supernatural, the paranormal, and anything to do with spirit. But I was ten years old when I really had my first in-my-face encounter with these natural, but mostly hidden forces.

My mother and I were going to the movies – I even remember what movie it was – Little Lord Fauntleroy (that will give you some idea of how old I am!) and yes, thank you, I remember enjoying it very much. But the real highlight of my day out with my mum happened even before we filed into the darkness of the movie theatre.

Having some time to fill before the movie started, we wandered along the road to a group of shops, one of which sold antiques. I loved antiques – I loved old stuff, period, so we went in.

The shop spread across two rooms, and when I glanced into the second room, my heart leapt. A matching pair of twin beds were set up in the middle of the room, complete with blankets and pillows tucked in against their carved headboards. I was smitten and already envisioning them in my bedroom at home as I made a beeline for them. There was no way I could ever convince my mum to buy them for me, but even at ten years old, a girl can dream, right?

Besides, they were gorgeous, and what I liked even more than old stuff, was gorgeous old stuff. My father, a cabinetmaker, had promised me a four-poster bed one day (cough cough it never happened) so I was primed towards bedroom furniture, I guess you could say.

I stopped dead still in my mad dash across the shop towards these beds. A couple metres from them and I was frozen, goose bumps pebbling my skin, and sucking air into my lungs through what suddenly felt like a soggy paper straw.

I remember my mother touching my arm and asking me what was wrong as I reversed my direction and began backing out of that second room, out of the whole shop in fact, to stand dazed on the footpath outside.

There was something wrong with those beds. I can still feel the darkness that clung to those bits of wood and springs. Looking at my mother I told her that something terrible had happened in those beds. I had no idea what, and I sure wasn't going to go back into that shop and wander up to the beds to take a closer look. All I knew – all I needed to know – was that something had happened involving that pair of beds, and that it hadn't been nice, and that whatever it was still clung to the furniture, seeped deep within the grain of the wood. I sure didn't want them anywhere near my comforting bedroom at home. I'd take my utilitarian little bed over those ones anytime at all.

Now, you may not go around about picking up on nasty left-over energy, but the fact is, in a world made of energy, it's everywhere, and some of it clings. Which is where the necessity for grounding, centering, and shielding ourselves comes in.

Have you ever gone to a busy mall a day or two before Christmas and come home frazzled and exhausted, even though you were only there for twenty minutes and you usually love shopping?

Have you ever been hiking and found a place to rest that you thought was completely beautiful, yet after a while found there was something unnerving and not quite right about the place?

And what about that one friend that we all have had at some stage – the one who seems to suck us dry when we visit, so that the first thing we do when we get home is have a nap?

We are receptive beings. Besides our physical body, we have an energetic one as well.

This part of us is constantly connecting with and feeling out the energy around us from people, places, things, the whole kit and caboodle. It's what allows us to appreciate atmosphere, it's the direct line to empathy, and it's how we feel essentially connected to our world.

But our energetic body also needs attention and protection, and just like we use soap and water to clean our face, we need to have some cleansing routines for our energetic selves too. Which is why we're going to learn some centring and grounding techniques. They're simple and effective, and mean that you won't get so clogged up with unwanted energy, and you'll be balanced and sure-footed. Which also means that you'll be healthier, feel less stressed, and more connected to the world in ways that are easy and joyous. No more carting around the accumulated energy of every person and place with which you come into contact.

Grounding, centring, and shielding are three different exercises, but they're all necessary and so complementary that when you do one, you'll often find yourself doing the others as well. As for grounding – well, the way I define it makes it pretty much a way of life.

It's also the foundation for doing magic. Walking steady and surefooted through the world is essential if you want to live magically, if you want to stretch your spirit in ways it is made to be stretched, if you want to connect easily every day to your spirit's path, and if you want to learn not to live in fear.

We are spiritual and physical beings here in this world – this world that also has a spiritual dimension, where everything is alive, where fairy races live almost unseen beside us.

To experience it all, to unlock our natural abilities, there are three things to my mind, that are essential practices enabling us to walk in flesh and spirit.

One of these is grounding, centring, and shielding.

Let's get started.

1

GROUNDING

THE CONCEPT BEHIND THIS IS SIMPLE. WE FLUSH away all the second-hand energy that we don't want clinging to us. Much like we wash our clothes to get rid of the stink of second-hand smoke, so do we want to clean ourselves of that energy.

We do this grounding by using what we have – and what do all of us have? The elemental forces that surround us – earth, air, fire, and water. We'll take the earth to begin with, as it's most commonly used when starting out, and for good reason: we stand, sit, and lie upon. It's big, solid, and porous. Perfect. It's also symbolically ideal, and when it comes to inner work – magical work, symbolism is a big thing. Symbolism is the language of the soul and uses simple images and ideas to communicate much larger ones. Once you step foot upon the path of spiritual growth and developing your inner world, of doing magic and being who and what you really are, symbolism is going to become your best friend.

So, grounding makes sense both in practical ways (that unwanted energy must go somewhere, and the earth is super convenient and one big recycling machine) and symbolically – being 'grounded' readies us for further experience.

Let's get to it, shall we? Here are the steps:

- Find somewhere to be steady where you won't be disturbed for a few minutes. You can stand, or sit, or lie down – whatever your physical condition allows and feels most right to you. Once you're good at this, you'll be able to do it anywhere anytime in practically the blink of an eye.

But for right now, if you're standing, begin with your feet comfortably about shoulder-width apart. Make sure you're well-balanced and steady. Let your arms hang loosely at your sides. Take a similar, relaxed posture if you're sitting or lying.

- Let yourself be aware of your breathing. Slow and deepen your breaths, calming and steadying yourself. Breathe slow and deep. Pay attention. Breath is the life of the world, a prayer, a spell, an incantation. Breathe in slowly, to the count of four. Hold it to the count of four, let it out, counting one, two, three, four. (If you feel short of breath when you're learning this technique, it helps to take a series of rapid breaths first, rather as though hyperventilating, to saturate yourself with oxygen).

- Close your eyes and focus inwards. Be still and let your attention mark how you are feeling. Mark how your body feels, its aches and pains, if any, its vitality, and strength. Seek then how your energy feels and describe it silently to yourself. Does it shift and flow freely through you? Or can you feel disruption, prickliness, the staticky discomfort of the unwanted energy?

- Underneath that disorganised, clingy energy, feel the strong, clean, and bright essence of your own self, your own energy. There will always be at least a thread of it there. Think of it as light, and send it downwards, out through both feet, and into the ground like roots. Now you are properly steady.

3

- It's time to move that unwanted energy. On your outward breaths, mentally push it downwards. Down through your body, down your legs, down into your 'roots' and out into the soil.

- Breathe slowly and deeply and expel the unwanted energy and emotions, clearing them down and out of your body.

- Feel yourself get lighter and brighter as you clear away all that unwanted energy.

THAT'S IT. THAT'S HOW GROUNDING IS DONE. Simple, right? No, it really is. There's no trick; it's just that easy.

Once we've done the grounding bit to get rid of accumulated and unwanted energy, most of us move straight into centring, which can also be done on its own, but should always be done after grounding.

Together, grounding and centring are about being clear, calm, and walking through the world balanced and certain.

Both are integral to our well-being. And to accessing our talents towards magic.

We're going to move onto centring in just a

moment, then shielding, and after that, we'll go deeper into all three – but first, a word about imagination.

Talk to anyone who does inner-world work, whether love and light, or witchcraft, and they'll all say the same thing – it begins with imagination.

Our minds are amazing things, which is good, because it's a complex world we live in, and there's a lot to navigate. Unfortunately, this complexity often means we can get a bit sceptical about things that look too easy. What? we ask – how can something be real just because we've imagined it? Well, think about it simplistically for a moment: everything that's anything you've ever done is a result of imagining beforehand. Maybe you called it planning instead, maybe you thought it was pretty spur of the moment, but really, even in that split second, you imagined it first and then ran with it. On an inner world level, imagination works even more directly, because imagination is not just well, imagination, but it's also the way we access our spirit. Imagining opens a door, and before you know it, you're through that door and doing that spiritual, magical thing.

So, when you're standing there imagining the energy flowing down your legs and into the ground, yes, it's really happening on that inner, energetic level, which is, of course, exactly where you need it to. The more you do it, the more the link between imagination and spirit strengthens, and then you're really cooking with gas.

And things that happen in the inner world have a direct effect on our outer perceptions, emotions, mindset, and often our physical body.

Which brings me to the word 'visualisation'. I think I've avoided it here so far, but you're going to come across it all the time when you're doing inner-world, magical work. Lots of you will have trouble with visualisation, because seeing pictures in our mind isn't something that comes naturally for everyone. Some of us imagine by hearing instead, some by feeling, and so on. I think the term 'visualisation' has become shorthand for whatever method your imagination best expresses itself. So, bear that in mind, and go with whatever works best for you.

Just breathe and try it, okay?

2

IN SHORT

- The constant, willy-nilly exchange of energy within every environment you find yourself is exhausting

- Extreme cases of uncleared energy in places and people can make them uncomfortable to encounter

- Grounding and centring help you avoid feeling overwhelmed

- It helps you avoid mistaking outside emotion and energy for your own (you get to stay balanced)

- It stops you from taking on the emotions of others (you won't be so easily influenced)

- It gives you a strong foundation for developing your inner world, which is essential if you want a spiritually, emotionally, and mentally healthy life

- Remember, you don't have to be psychic to be affected by energy – we all absolutely are (of course, if you're an empath, you really need to know this stuff)

3

CENTRING

You've all heard, I'm sure, talk of 'being centred', and 'finding your centre'. This is exactly what we're going to do, but instead of just thinking about it in some abstract (and wishful, more often than not) way, we're going to actually do it.

Centring goes hand in hand with grounding, and you should do both together, but centring can be done on its own. I spend most of my time navigating between the mundane world and the Otherworld – that of spirit, so being centred is something I strive to be constantly, because magic really can't be done without being centred, without knowing where you are and who you are. It is a way of being in the world that becomes the foundation of every other practice you wish to have. It is also the state of being that opens you up to your soul's path and puts you in line with the flow of energy through the universe. And when you're in flow with the world, with your own purpose, well, that's when you can really step into your magic.

Centring is also vital for whenever you're feeling stressed or under pressure. It's the to-do thing for when you're out and about and getting tired, or when you need an extra dose of patience, or simply when you want to ramp up your energy level to perform at your best. It's about being focused and still relaxed, and there's nothing quite like it for making you feel calm, confident, and super-capable. In other words, learn how to do it, and do it every day!

In essence, centring is two things:

- moving your personal energy to a strong centre, so that you're neither too heavy (bogged down) or too light (up in the clouds)

- a focusing and acknowledgement of the fact that you are more than flesh and blood, that you are in fact made of soul energy as well and as such are capable of amazing feats of perspective and magic.

Let's get to it:

- Stand or sit or lie down – whichever is easiest for your physical condition

⊥ so that you are balanced and steady.

- Breathe slowly, deeply, paying attention to the physical sensations of your body, of the room you're in, of the world outside that room, and inside yourself to your own breath, the rush of your own blood, the beat of your heart, the flow of energy through your body, the wafting of your aura around the outside of your physical body. Breathe in slowly, to the count of four, hold it to the count of four, exhale, one, two, three, four.

- Close your eyes, focus inward, go through the grounding exercise if you wish to. Breathe slowly, calmly.

- Feel your own energy, that calm, steady strength of it. Feel how it is inside your body, and also outside of it. Feel the way it tingles in the air outside your physical body.

- Breathe in, and with your breath, imagine drawing in clean, clear light through the top of your head. Allow it to flow into you, down into every limb, from head to toe, and through your aura as well, until all of you is bright and glowing. You can visualise (see) this, or feel it, or talk yourself through it with your inner voice, or just simply know that it is happening – whatever suits you best. During this, however, stay open to feeling this sensation of light and energy in your body.

- Lift your arms to the sky and stretch upwards. If you cannot lift your arms, feel yourself stretching upwards. Imagine that the light is streaming into you from the sky, through your fingers, your hands, down your arms, into your head and into your body, streaming down through you and into the ground on which you are so sturdily planted.

- Rooted to earth, stretched to the sky, feel yourself an essential bridge between the two. Let the energy flow in and through you.

- Once you have this energy streaming into you, flowing through and around you, take a deep breath and bring your hands down until you are cupping them together in front of you, at the navel point –

your cauldron – as though you are holding some of the energy you've accessed, and then turn your hands and press the light into yourself, into your centre.

- Allow the bright, clear energy to spread into and outwards from this area, so that now it is not flowing through you, but flowing from you, from a nice, strong centre, illuminating you and your aura.

Done! Now you really know why it's called centring!

4

IN SHORT

- Grounding and centring make use of your imagination to affect your energetic body

- They use the elements as stabilising factors, and both earth and sky as a source of energy flow

- Grounding draws on metaphors of steadiness, clarity, and steadfastness

- Centring draws on concepts of feeling and balanced and radiant

- Language and symbolism (metaphors) and visualisation and imagination are used in inner world exercises

- Inner world exercises have a reality that is felt on all our levels of being

- These exercises are the foundation for learning and performing acts of magic

5

SHIELDING

So, NOW THAT WE KNOW HOW TO KEEP ourselves nicely balanced and grounded, getting rid of all that unwanted second-hand energy, and recharging our own batteries, let's look at something that takes those two lessons a step further.

Yep, we're talking about shielding. Because while disposing of that sticky, uncomfortable energy by grounding is an essential skill, wouldn't it also be super-useful to know how to avoid picking up all that second-hand energy in the first place?

It would, and it is, and the technique is called shielding. It's exactly what it sounds like – a method of protecting yourself from unwanted energy. And just like grounding and centring, it's simple to learn.

Shielding allows you to surround yourself with a barrier of your own protective energy. This barrier keeps you from absorbing the energy in the environment around you, whether that second-hand energy is coming from a person, a place, or a build-up of old emotion that hasn't been cleared away (we'll talk more about that in a future guide).

We all are probably aware of having a sensation of 'personal space'. It's that bubble of space around us that gets to feeling uncomfortable when someone steps into it. We've all had those people who stand too close when they're talking to us, to the point that it can feel pretty creepy – that's your personal space they're intruding upon, and it's this personal space that we build a shield around in this technique.

Take a moment right now and see if you can feel this personal comfort zone of yours. With all the grounding and centring exercises you've been doing – or will be doing when you've finished reading this little book – you will get to the point that you can feel your own energy and the way it extends outside of your physical body. Make it something of a habit to become aware of it, so that you know what your own energy feels like in all sorts of situations, when you're at rest, for example, when you're agitated, and when you're blissing out. Being aware of your own energy is step one of being able to manipulate it, so go ahead and practice.

But back to shielding. This bubble of personal space is basically your aura. That's the energy you're experiencing when you're aware of it extending outside of your body. Your aura is all about your personal space. It's your very personal boundary, and it's the space you take up energetically, emotionally, and spiritually.

Shielding allows us to protect ourselves from sensory overload, and if you're especially open to the emotions of others, then it's another essential skill to learn. While the ability to touch the emotional energy of others, and the residual energy of places and things is valuable if those are areas you want to work in, you still need to learn to regulate how much you take in, so you can be safe, and so that your interactions with outside energy don't overwhelm you. After all, you're not going to be much use to your distraught friend if you're climbing the walls because you can feel her distress so keenly, and similarly, you're not going to be able to energetically assess situations of any sort if you are swamped by whatever is hanging about.

(Just a quick note here – you might think that shielding sounds like the most important exercise ever, but don't think to do it at the expense of grounding, and particularly, centring. Centring is the essential tool, because it will strengthen your spirit to the point, that if you want to do certain types of spirit work at a high level, you'll be able to – and need to – lower any shields and still be strong enough at your centre to not be in danger).

Importantly too, gaining control over your own energy and boundaries means that with practice you will be able to raise and lower your shields with a simple thought, allowing you to develop your inner world much more efficiently, and growing your connection with all spirit. Which is, in my opinion, the ultimate goal for all of us – reconnecting with our own soul, and living with deep, spiritual purpose and intention. That's real magic.

So how do we do this shielding thing?

- Stand, sit, or lie loosely and comfortably, steady upon the earth, hands relaxed at your sides.

- Go through your grounding and centring process. Use your imagination to direct your energy, knowing that what you are doing is real, that you are indeed moving and connecting with energy.

- Quietly, raise your awareness of your own bubble of energy that surrounds you. If it helps, you can give it a colour, or texture.

- Hold your awareness of it there in your mind and open yourself to feeling it physically as well. Feel your aura as a slight tingling in the air around you, and as a pressure in the area at your navel (where you did your centring) that spreads out all around you from that point. Use as many senses as you can to experience your aura this way.

- Your aura will, at this stage, be free-floating around you, the edges not defined. Giving it definition and a boundary edge is the next step, and it's what shielding is.

- Imagine your aura with a defined edge. Give it a shape or form. Use whatever symbol seems natural to you. You could make your aura into an actual bubble (my personal method), or a shell or egg of some sort – whatever works, as long as it completely encloses you.

- Remember, that your imagination is your own tool, so do what is comfortable for you, imagining that you have a boundary of some sort surrounding you, made from your own energy extending from your centre.

- Make it see-through so you don't get claustrophobic!

There you have it. That's how you use your

energy to shield yourself from outside influences. Like everything we've talked about, it will take practice, so add it to your daily grounding and centring routine until you can do it with the flip of a mental switch.

Speaking of mental switches, there's a nifty trick you can do while visualising your bubble shield, that will strengthen the experience, and make it easier to do. This involves adding in a physical gesture to reinforce the mental and energetic exercise you are doing.

Your physical cue can be anything you like, although I very much recommend that you make it something unobtrusive, since most of the time when you're out and about and need to shield yourself, you're not going to want to draw attention to the fact that you're doing magical stuff.

Yes, you did read that right. What you're doing here is magic, which is defined as using the will to effect change in your environment. Your will is flexed by means of the imagination, and in this case the effect on your environment is not to be inundated with its unwanted energy.

Hand gestures have always played a big part in various magical methodologies. You could spend some time down a nice rabbit hole researching them, and maybe you want to before choosing one that makes sense for you to use in your shielding practice.

In the meantime, here are a few suggestions for your first magical gesture:

- Press your hands together over your centre. This is a reminder of where your energy for the shield is coming from. You could also turn your hands palm out afterwards, and make a brief pushing motion outward with them, just as though you were extending the energy out to your boundary. This is a good one to start your practice with, as it is an active illustration of what you are doing. It is, however, a little obtrusive for public use, so after a while you'll probably develop a less noticeable, shorthand version.

- Touching finger and thumb together on one hand. This is a really simple gesture but is big on symbolism. You're making a circle with your finger and thumb and it's a good shorthand way of acknowledging that you are not only centring yourself in the whole cosmos (the circle is a symbol for the cosmos) but also that you are centred in your shield. I believe if you touch your ring finger to your thumb, you're also making the sign of the mudra, a

sacred hand gesture in Hinduism.
It's certainly a discreet and
appropriate gesture you might find
suits you.

- Touch a hand to your forehead. I
  don't use physical gestures very
  often anymore, but this one is my
  personal preference. Like the other
  gestures, it's a cue that speaks to our
  spirit – the part of ourselves to
  whom energy work is second nature.
  I use this one of touching fingers to
  forehead as a way of
  acknowledgement. It reminds me
  that what I am doing is real,
  effective, and has consequences (in
  this case, the consequence is
  protection). I also use it in other
  situations where acknowledgement
  and gratitude is needed. But it
  definitely works as a cue for
  shielding too.

- Make the sign of the cross, or four
  directions. Again, whether used in
  the Catholic or Pagan consciousness,
  this is a gesture of both blessing and
  centring. As such, it works perfectly.

- Touching a talisman. Many of us
  wear pendants and other pieces of

jewellery for more than the purposes of adornment. Putting your fingers to a pendant, crystal, or talisman (and one piece can be all three, or a combination) is an excellent cue to focus your attention on shielding. If you go with this option, then it might be nice to choose a piece specifically to use for this purpose. As you use it again and again, it becomes imbued with your directed energy, and amplifies it back at you when you make the gesture. Simply make sure you look after it, and keep its energy clean and purposeful (which means keeping its purpose in mind every time you handle it, and following good practices for looking after ritual objects – which I guess is a whole 'nother book).

Now you know how to ground, centre, and shield yourself, and you're practicing it, hopefully every day.

6

IN SHORT

- During grounding, we clear our energetic body of unwanted energy

- During centring, we rebalance and replenish our own energy

- During shielding, we reinforce our boundaries so as not to let unwanted outside energy in, and to keep our own energy from leaking outwards.

7

ENERGY WORK

NOW YOU'VE THE BASICS DOWN, AND REALLY soon you'll be terrific at it, incorporating it into your regular daily practices.

So, is there anything else to do, or is that it?

We've gone through the essentials of all three exercises, but you bet there's more. Because as with most things, there's basic, and then there's fancy.

When you're working with imagery and symbolism in terms of your inner world, you're likely to want to find more resonant methods than just the basic bare-bones method of, well, anything really. So, let's look at some advanced ways of grounding, centring, and shielding. It will be fun, and the more you stretch yourself in this way, the better you'll be at it all, the deeper your inner world will be, and the more connected you'll feel, to yourself, and the world, both physical and spirit.

Energy is a potent thing. It affects us emo-

tionally and physically. Everything has energy –
you'll know that yourself from those times
when you've had a brilliant idea or scheme, and
all of a sudden you feel full of life and everything is vibrant and the world looks like it's full
of endless possibilities. When you're setting off
on an adventure, you're energised, rearing to
go, the mental and emotional (and spiritual)
stimulation sends energy surging through you.
All this is great, especially if you have the disci-
pline to channel that energy where it needs to
go, and the ability to pace yourself, not allowing
that burst of good feeling and energy to be only
that – a burst – but instead to use it to keep you
going over the whole course of your adventure
or project. Because a burst, or even just the
build-up of excited energy, is exciting when
you're in the midst of it but exhausting when it
drains away, and you're left feeling deflated and
tired.

This is not just second-hand energy we're
talking about here, but the energy we ourselves
produce. If you can pick up on other people's
energy, you can bet you're producing it yourself.

During times of great activity, excitement,
and very often when we're starting down new
paths, we tend to produce an over-abundance
of energy, which if we don't manage properly
can lead us into firstly manic activity, then exhaustion. I have spent years learning to manage
my energy, keeping it within sensible boundaries. I used to be fairly impulsive, swinging be-

tween periods of elation and exhaustion. Finally, I recognised that while it was actually pretty fun living like this, it was too unpredictable and tiring for me to achieve my goals, particularly my work goals, with any consistency. Thus, I learnt to regulate myself, smoothing out the highs – and the lows as well – to become far more even-tempered, productive, and focused.

But even so, life throws spanners in the works, and sets us big and little challenges. How we navigate through these contributes to our growth mentally, emotionally, and spiritually. It's all connected.

Not all these life events need to be 'bad' to mean that we have to deal with ourselves on an energetic level. When I met my wife, we were living in different countries, and while we had lots of plans, for both work and life, they necessarily had to wait until we were both in the same physical place.

You might be able to imagine that this brought with it all sorts of energetic issues. Anticipation and excitement combined with frustration and enforced patience had me running on super high-octane gasoline. It wasn't sustainable.

I had to do something with all this extra energy. I had already extended my physical routine in the hope that more exercise would help. It did, but as I do most of my planning and creative work during physical exercise, it wasn't quite as useful as I'd hoped – the energy I was grounding by exerting myself physically was simply coming back around again because I was also mentally more active and excited.

Greater measures needed to be taken. As I was working deeply at the time on magical, inner-world levels, it was a natural step to deal with this energy issue by extending my grounding and centring routine. And because I'd been doing the grounding and centring thing for years, coming up with the extra steps was instinctive, just like it will be for you when you're practiced. Develop your spirit and it feeds you.

I do a lot of journeying to the Otherworld and have done for most of my life. The Otherworld place in which I do most of my spirit work is a forest, and I feel very closely aligned with trees. All of us have lessons we can learn from trees, and I decided I was going to take a leaf (or branch?) from their book to deal with my excess energy issue.

Firstly, I picked a place that existed in my physical world, that echoed the forested inner landscape I was familiar with. I didn't physically go there, although if you're going to do this exercise, I would recommend actually going to the place you pick, at least the first time.

I imagined myself standing in this place. It's a grassy clearing beside a river that runs shallow, but swift and clear, tumbling and rushing over some rocks not far from the clearing. Trees hang over the water as though trying to see their reflections and climb the steep hills that rise all around. It's beautiful here, filled with that combination of activity and serenity that nature is so good at. I planted my feet firmly on the grass and breathed deeply of the air, smelling the soil, the water, the heat of the sun.

Lifting my arms, I spread them wide, reaching my fingertips into the breeze, digging my toes like roots into the soil, connecting with sun and sky and soil, becoming one with the earth and sky, balanced, poised.

I was humming with energy, my own over-load of it, and as I connected with my sur-roundings, tree and river and earth and sky came alive and we were all there together, equal companions, ready and willing to work together.

'Give your unwanted energy to me,' said the earth. 'Let me take it for you so you can be bal-anced.' I gave it to the earth, letting it pour from me deep into the soil under my feet, feeling it tingle inside me from outstretched fingers, from the top of my head, sending it down into the ground, feeling it spread out there, held by the earth.

'If you need any of it back,' the earth told me then, 'you've only to walk consciously, and draw it back with each step.' Now that was in-teresting. The earth was offering not only to take the energy I didn't need, but to feed it back to me whenever I should need it. Energetically being a source of strength and stability, as well as physically.

I finished the exercise by centring myself between earth and sky, drawing my energy to my centre and stabilizing myself. Opening my eyes, I felt extraordinarily calm and self-possessed. There was no longer that feeling of manic excitement like I'd stuck my finger in an electric socket. I was no longer fizzing and sparking. Instead I was well, clear, and centred.

The use of the natural world like this is terrifically effective for grounding and centring exercises. Particularly, there's something about using elemental forces that super-charges the whole thing. So, let's go through a bunch of examples and you can try them all out, and pick one or maybe even more that particularly resonate with you.

8

GROUNDING WITH THE ELEMENTS

Grounding with Earth

THIS IS THE ULTIMATE GROUNDING/STEADYING element since we spend all our time walking and balancing ourselves upon the earth. Use it to your advantage, and as you can see from my story above, the spirit of earth (and every element) is more than willing to work with you.

Possibly the easiest way to clear your energy specifically with earth, is to imagine yourself a tree, as I did. Trees are deeply rooted in the earth, as well as naturally reaching to the sky, which gives you twice the bang for your buck.

Or you could imagine yourself standing or walking on any piece of ground that suits you. We once had a small, dormant volcano sitting a few hundred metres from our back porch, and a fun grounding exercise was to imagine walking up its flanks and letting my energy flow and mingle with its own. Try doing this exercise (minus the sleeping volcano unless you also happen to have one handy) by physically walking while you visualise yourself connecting with the earth underfoot and giving your energy into the soil. It's effective, and it's also invigorating.

This combination of physically doing a thing while energetically doing your ritual is fundamental to inner-world, magical practice. The more you can ritualise your practices in this way, the more effective they will be. What we are really trying to achieve in the big picture, is the exercise and acknowledgement of spirit. Gear all your practices towards this, and you will, quite honestly, be transformed.

One summer when I was in my twenties, I decided that I would walk barefoot as often as possible. I did so, doing it as a magical practice, being mindful every time I walked that I was grounding myself, exchanging my energy with that of the earth beneath me, and connecting to the earth's spirit in a way that woke my own to greater awareness. That was the summer when the magic really kicked up a gear in my life. On top of all the other things I'd been doing, some of them for years, that one thing more opened a door to magic in a way I'm still reaping the rewards of almost thirty years later.

With that in mind, you can think of all sorts of ways of grounding your energy with earth.

Fashion things out of clay while sending your energy into the medium. Get your hands dirty in the garden while going through your exercises. Or perhaps even put aside a particular tray or pot of soil that you can dip your hands into while consciously clearing and grounding yourself. Really, you're limited only by imagination and inclination.

Grounding with Water

This method is an easy thing to fit into a daily routine since we all wash ourselves every day. Water cleans and clears, and in the case of rivers, creeks, streams, and showers, it flows. That flowing can wash away your unwanted energy, leaving you squeaky clean energetically as well as physically.

I'm sure you can figure out how to do an easy cleansing ritual while in the shower, using your imagination and your growing visualisation skills. But it doesn't have to be a shower. Fill a basin with water and ritually dip your hands into it. By 'ritually' I mean doing it with intention, acknowledging both your spirit and the spirit of the water (I'm an animist which means that I live in deep awareness that all things have spirit and sovereignty). You may even find it helps your focus to speak while you do it. To describe and order the process. It can be as simple as saying 'I wash away that which is unneeded', or as involved as you're feeling inspired to get. You could do a fun grounding and centring ritual sometimes when it is raining. Go outside in the rain (not during a thunderstorm, though, okay?) and let nature work with you. Go through your routine, imagining the rain taking your unwanted energy with it and washing it into the ground underfoot. Just remember that whichever method you use, it requires more than just the physical gestures – there must be the inner work too, the intention, the imagination. You have to direct your will; you must make something happen. And by using your imagination, combining it with gesture and symbolism, your spirit will come to the party and make it happen. Everything works together because everything is connected. – Don't forget too, to give your thanks to whatever element you are using. Remember, all things have spirit, not just you.

Grounding with Air

I'm sure you're getting the idea now and maybe you've even picked a couple methods to try yourself. I personally like working with air, as for some reason a cold wind – of which there are a lot far down in the southern hemisphere where I live – opens me up and spreads me wide to the world of spirit. I'm quite sure a hot wind would do the same, but one of you will have to let me know about that one.

We are not separate from nature, but an integral part of it. It is only ourselves who set us apart from the world around us. We are soul-aspects who have come to this place and time, this world of earth and water, air and fire, to be part of it, to align with its spirit and physicality, and to learn from the experience. Let's make the most of it.

Stand outside in a good wind; face it and spread your arms wide to embrace it. Feel it buffeting against you, let it in to become a part of you. Let it force the cobwebs from deep inside you, cleaning and clearing and waking you up. Let it take your troubles and anxieties and blow them away. Become literally, your own breath of fresh air.

Grounding with Fire

Fire is no gentle thing. It burns, reduces to ash and bone, so for cleansing purposes, it's probably the one to use when you've something particular you want to clear away, and you know the name of this thing. It's particularly good to use in times of transition – when you want to mark the movement from one state of being to another. That way you can light a fire, and ritually burn the old, outgrown energy, clearing the way for your new growth and modes of living.

In a gentler way, using candles to focus would work well, and can be a regular way to focus for cleansing and centring. By lighting a candle and going through your cleansing routine while aligned in spirit and focus to the gentle flame, you can achieve very good results, imagining that you are part of this gentle flame, and that it is burning away the unwanted energy, leaving you clear and revived for another day.

9

IN SHORT

- You can add in other aspects to your grounding and centring rituals to make them more vivid for yourself

- Using the elements of earth, water, air, and fire are easy and effective ways to achieve this

- You are really limited only by your imagination when devising your own routines and rituals

- Combining physical movement with your symbolism and visualisation strengthens the exercises

- You are achieving real results even though you are using only inner resources, perhaps combined with outside ritual. It's still real.

- You can design different grounding and centring rituals for different purposes, to mark transitions, for those times you need something more powerful, as part of a regular cycle, for example to enhance your spiritual self-care.

10

ADVANCED SHIELDING

WE'VE GONE THROUGH SOME EXTRA METHODS OF grounding and centring, and now we're going to talk some more about shielding, and develop some advanced techniques.

Shielding is a little more involved than grounding and centring, since you're not just moving energy, you're manipulating it for a particular purpose – in this case, to protect yourself from unwanted influences.

There are going to be times however, more often than not probably, when you don't want to close yourself off completely from the energetic environment around you. Surely there's a way to continuing protecting yourself, while still being able to experience and process the energy around you? To get the measure of it so that you are fully aware of your surroundings (always a good idea) and take appropriate actions, whatever they may be?

There is, of course, and we're going to call it

'filtering' since that is exactly what it is. In shielding, we create a protective shell of our energy, so that nothing can get in, or out. Filtering allows us to make this barrier selective, one that enables us to interact under controlled circumstances with outside energy.

Think of it this way – with the shield, we have transformed our energy into a solid barrier, through which we cannot be touched, and through which we also cannot reach. You can see that this would be useful when you want to move through a situation or place impervious to the energy in it. When we filter our shield, we create one that is made of more porous material, so that there is some energy can come through, and some of ours can go out.

Even more brilliantly, when we get good at filtering, we can vary the degree and direction of this energy exchange. We can make it so that we can allow a measure of outside energy in so that we can get a taste of how disruptive or otherwise it is, and we can let some of our own outwards, or we can keep it all inside our filtering barrier. It all depends on the situation we find ourselves in.

This is incredibly useful, as weird as you might be thinking it sounds. But let's think for a moment, of some of the situations in which it might be a good idea. Remember that story I told you at the beginning of this book – about the beds in the antique shop? If I'd known then what I do now, I would have been able to put up a shield, so as not to be completely blown away by the strength of the psychic impressions radiating from those old beds, and then I could have set my filters so that I could 'reach out' and experience a dialled down amount of that energy, and get more of an idea, under safer conditions, of what exactly was going on with them.

For those of us who have any sort of psychic gifts, or are in any way empathic, learning this filtering technique is imperative. It will allow you to significantly lessen your chances of being overwhelmed and enable you to explore and use your gifts much more effectively. Valerie, my wife, and I both have extremely high antennas, psychically, and as such we also find it incredibly easy to 'tune in' to each other's emotional wavelengths. As we've also done a lot of healing work together, and for each other, this has been super helpful, but we definitely had to learn filtering so as not to be overwhelmed. When you can feel another's emotions that strongly – and a lot of you empaths will be able to relate to this – it's very hard not to let them take you over and become your own emotions as well. Shielding and filtering completely solves the problem, and because you can adjust your filtering levels, you can still empathise with someone, feeling what they are going through so that you can more deeply understand it, but not so much that it takes you over.

Filtering is a sophisticated method of working with energy, but it's also simple to do. As you have seen with all the work we've done so far, the way to manipulate energy is through the use of your imagination and will. Which means every single one of us can do it. Even if you don't consider yourself a particularly imaginative person, I'll bet you are a lot more so than you think, and that with a bit of practice, you'll be great at it.

So, let's get to it. How do we turn our bubble of energy shield into a smooth filtering machine?

Because we're learning, we're going to run through the whole practice in a formal way. When you've got it down doing it like this, then it's time to practice it in different situations. More on that later though. Let's just get started.

- Stand, sit, or lie comfortably, depending on your physical ability. Breath slowly, deeply, calmly. Let your body be as loose and relaxed as possible.

- Go through your grounding and centring routine. When you get to the centring, and you're holding your energy at your centre – that point under your rib cage – and letting it infuse your whole body, then pause for a moment.

43

- Push that energy outwards until it envelopes your whole body for a distance of approximately 50cm to a metre (about a foot to two and a half feet) and define the boundaries of it until they feel solid and secure. This is your shield, and you're pretty good at making it now. (Practice holding your arms out to your sides with palms facing one another - now, move your hands towards each other and feel where that energy begins).

- Hold that shield in place. You've been practicing this, and it's a lot like any exercise – you must develop your muscles. Here you're developing your mental and energetic muscles. You're stretching your spirit.

- Now that your shield is nice and steady, imagine the barrier more porous. Imagine that it is made of something that is translucent, or breathes, or anything at all that works for you that allows air (energy) through in small amounts.

- Hold your shield with this filter in place. Concentrate on being able to

feel the energy outside of yourself,
in varying degrees.

What does this feel like, you're asking? Okay. All along when you've been doing these exercises, you've been taking note of what each feel like. (Right? If you haven't, then go back and do them paying close attention to the sensations in your body, and also how it feels in your mind. That's awesome!). Here's what they feel like to me:

When I'm grounding, I'm first aware of the unwanted energy inside and swirling around me. This is why I'm doing the exercise in the first place – because the feeling is uncomfortable. It's all staticky, and buzzing. It makes you want to shake it off, and it almost sets your teeth on edge. It's that feeling that makes you irritable and snappy. That drains and tires you. The one that makes you feel like you need to scrape all this unseen muck off you. Almost like when you've eaten too much sugar and you've got a big sugar rush, which is not really all that comfortable.

Moving all this energy down and into the ground is a relief. I feel lighter as soon as it starts draining away and I'm sure you do too. Since I'm also seeing it as light as well as energy, it's a relief to be rid of that sticky dark stuff. Lifting my arms to the sky and bringing down bright, clear energy into myself first makes me feel almost like I am melting with relief as it flows into me, clean and cleansing. By the time I'm on to the centring part, I'm feeling invigorated, and that energy is crisp and purposeful, and deeply connected with all the beauty of the world. I can feel that beauty, deep in my body, and my mind. Barriers are down, the debris of the world cleared away, and I'm feeling bright and alive and part of everything. That staticky feeling is gone, and now the energy has a clear humming feel to it.

Holding a shield up is an interesting feeling. During centring, your barriers are down – which is the major reason why we practice it somewhere we won't be disturbed, and where we already feel safe. So, move from being 'open' during centring, to being 'closed' inside your shield. You should be able to feel the difference.

I feel it as a definite sensation of self-containment. I can see the world, I can reach out and touch it, smell it, feel the movement of the breeze and the people walking by, but we are not connected. I move through the world in a bubble. It feels very much like having one of your senses switched off, which in truth of course, it is.

Which brings up an important point. Enclosed in an impermeable bubble is not how you want to go through the world. It might seem a good idea on the face of it, since the world is such a noisy, chaotic place, but we are not designed to be disconnected from it. And that noise and chaos can be managed – and the best ways to do so are by strengthening your spirit through these exercises, and by filtering.

We're back at filtering again – how about that? So, if being completely shielded feels like being closed off behind safety glass, how do we know when we are filtering properly? What does that feel like?

FILTERING CARRIES THE SENSATIONS OF BEING protected, and in a quiet space that dampens the noise of outside energy, but it doesn't have that self-contained, closed off feeling to it. Instead, it feels controlled – and who doesn't like the sensation of being in control? The bubble barrier is thinner, and you feel like you've relaxed a little, and the world is a little closer, so that you can reach out and touch it if you want. When you nudge up alongside someone else, you can feel dimly the swirling of their energy, and its flavour. If theirs is pleasant, you can open up a little more, and connect energetically with them without being swamped, and if it's the opposite, overwhelming or dark, you can judge that and decide what you want to do from there.

You can also choose how much you radiate out into the world, and believe me, if you practice these exercises enough, your spirit will radiate, and you will be able to turn it up and down like a lamp, depending on your circumstances, and how you want to interact with the world and with others at any given moment.

Shielding and filtering is all about connecting safely with the energy that is always around you. It allows you to respond in varying degrees as it suits you, from opening up completely to closing off and repelling directly.

I was in a situation several years ago that I'd always known was possible, but wasn't one I usually encountered at the time, in which the ability to shield competently saved me from an uncomfortable situation. I was doing some distance healing work, which was at the time a new skill I was developing. It came naturally, but it was still new. I was in my own home, physically relaxed in a safe space while on a spirit level I had connected with the person with whom I was working and operating in that sphere, when suddenly a spirit hurtled towards me at racing speed. It was completely unexpected and happened incredibly fast. One moment I was doing my thing, and then next something (someone) was zooming towards me with the intention of latching on.

Luckily, I've been practicing these centring, shielding, and filtering methods I'm teaching you for a very long time, and without even conscious thought (there wasn't even time for that) I had thrown up my shield in a flare of bright silver fire and sent that spirit careening off, having likely shocked it insensible. All this happened in the merest blink of an eye, but it certainly reinforced the importance in yet another way, of being able to shield yourself.

While you likely will not have to use these techniques for psychic self-defence, learning them will strengthen your spirit and connection, and allow you to navigate your way through the outer, everyday world with greater confidence. Keeping an eye on your energy and making sure it's clean and healthy will positively affect your life in a multitude of ways.

I ONCE SAID IN A POST ON INSTAGRAM:

"So, you want to know how to develop your intuition?

Here are my top five suggestions (more like requirements, actually):

1. Don't watch so much TV

2. Choose and limit carefully your online activities

3. Get out into nature

4. Remember and work with your dreams.

5. Learn grounding and centring techniques."

I REALLY DO THINK THAT GROUNDING AND centring, along with shielding and filtering, are foundational methods for working with energy;

and working with energy is itself the basis for expanding your inner world and facilitating connection with the universe and spirit. In other words, it's pretty much essential if you want a connected, magical life.

Once you're used to practicing these techniques in your own undisturbed space, then it's time to take your show on the road. Fortunately, it's the sort of work that you can do unobtrusively, without anyone noticing what you're up to. Even if you've chosen to incorporate gestures into your routine, you can still centre and shield yourself without anyone raising an eyebrow. The key is practice.

Start when you're still on your own and unlikely to be disturbed, but this time do it sitting down at the breakfast table, your cup of coffee in front of you. Centre and shield yourself when you're taking the dog for a walk. Once you've got the hang of it in different situations, take it another step further.

Centre and shield yourself when you're on the bus or train. Instead of only doing it when the dog is the only nearby critter, practice it when you're walking down a busy street, when you're waiting in line at Starbucks, and when you're flinging around a frisbee at the dog park.

The next and last step is, of course, to go even further, and do the whole routine when you're actually interacting with someone. This is the tricky one, but don't worry. It can be done. Your mind is a clever thing, and you can project and maintain your shield with the back part of your mind, while paying attention to your companion with the front. You might be asked the first few times why you're so distracted, but you'll get better at it so that it's really not noticeable.

Once you've learnt to hold your shield in place when you're talking to someone, play around with your filtering levels. After all, you're sitting right opposite someone who, chances are, has their own energy spilling out willy nilly, so it's the perfect opportunity to experiment with tuning into their energy, and tuning it out, to feel what it's like, while taking care not to go swimming around in it.

11

IN SHORT

- Filtering enables you to adjust your interaction with energy

- Filtering means that you can still work with outside energy, but you won't get overwhelmed by it

- You will be able to protect yourself, but remain aware of what's going on energetically, outside of yourself

- Filtering gives you choices about how you will move through situations and events

- Filtering allows you to remain empathic while protecting yourself from overwhelm

- Filtering means that you can protect yourself from negative energy while still dealing with it.

12

CONNECTING WITH ENERGY

I SHOULD PROBABLY BE ENDING THIS LITTLE GUIDE at the end of the last section, but I can't resist adding one more exercise for you to do. You see, what is grounding, centring, and shielding yourself, if you also do not learn to connect with the energy of the very world in which you walk?

We do not live on this earth separate from it. Or at least, we shouldn't. We are an intrinsic part of the natural world, of the spirit of the world, and as such, I think it is important to acknowledge this, and live consciously as such.

There is nothing in this world and the Otherworld which does not have life (spirit) and I do think that an important part of our work here in this lifetime, and all our lifetimes, is to work not only for the good of our own soul, but for the good of the earth, and each other, and for every living thing. We must not only strive for wholeness for ourselves, but for all those with whom we share this world.

It is past time for all of us to walk in awareness of the living energy of the ground we walk upon, and the spirit that infuses everything surrounding us. The earth is badly out of balance, and that means that we in turn can never quite be in balance.

But to be in a position to do what we can in these circumstances, we must be as healthy as possible. We are biological as well as spirit beings, so we must eat well, sleep and exercise well, taking care of our physical vehicles to the best of our abilities, whether we have chronic illnesses or not. (An interesting side-note – some of history's best spiritual mediums and magical practitioners suffered from chronic illnesses; speculation on this fact could take us down some fascinating rabbit holes).

So, since energy can be felt all through your nervous system, look after your nervous system. Quit smoking, quit drinking, taking drugs. Be mindful that driving these bodies we're in is difficult at the best of times, so better we learn where all the pedals are. It's impossible to deal with the trials and stresses of life if we are dislocated, anxious, and not fully in our bodies or on the ground. We must cultivate calmness, presence, and focus. To do this, we must be as stable as possible in our bodies.

This is why grounding and centring are so important, why breathing properly is important

– not only does it flex and stretch our spirits, but it means that we sit more comfortably in our bodies, and will not become light-headed, flighty, panicked, and out of control.

Balance in this, as everything, is important. We do not want to become hyper-vigilant, which is another increasing side effect of this world and the trauma many of us experience. We want instead to be calm and observant, and we can do this by being grounded and centred, and always bringing ourselves back to this state – time after time after time in the course of a day, if necessary. This practice will have so many flow-on effects, you'll barely recognise yourself after a time of making this state of being your default position.

Here are some questions for you to consider, and afterwards, I'll give you another exercise.

Being in your body

- How aware are you, generally, of being in your body?

- Where are you focused? Are you adrift in your imagination, always away on a flight of fancy?

- Or are you stuck in your own head, always thinking, and calculating?

Being on the earth

- How aware are you of being on the earth?

- How aware are you of your immediate environment?

Being in your breath

- Is your breathing generally erratic, or calm and steady?

- Are you willing to practice slow, considered breathing? (breathing in to the count of 4-6, holding it to same count, exhaling to count of 4-6).

I recently spent almost a year in another country, a lot of that time in less than comfortable circumstances. I was very aware of being in a geographically foreign land. It felt different, and the difference sat heavily on me, even while I was enjoying the adventure of seeing new places and meeting new people. I lost track of where each direction was because it wasn't what I was used to (particularly going from the Southern Hemisphere where I live to the Northern where everything is upside down).

I could feel the land, and having lived on an island, even a large island such as New Zealand, the sheer size and weight of continental America was hugely different and uncomfortable. Extending my senses, I recognised nothing. To one side of me, there was an immense stretch of land like nothing I'd experienced before. It felt like it went on so far, so very, very far. And so many people! When I stretched my spirit to taste it, to feel it out, there were so many people, so much noise, so much activity. I've spent time in the United Kingdom before, but that's an island too – nothing like America.

It was disconcerting. Even the ocean felt different.

It's important to ground ourselves where we live. To become familiar with our geography, to belong, like a tree, where we are planted. To recognise, when we reach out with our senses, the land around us. The hills, mountains, plains, rivers, streams, cities, the weight and life of the very land that sustains us.

We can not afford to be disconnected from the land. It needs us, and we need it. Ours is a symbiotic relationship, and so far, we have not honoured that relationship. We have done worse than that – we have plundered and pillaged and raped. It needs to change.

And it changes first and foremost with each one of us, individually.

. . .

- Be relaxed in a quiet place where you won't be disturbed. Run through your grounding and centring rituals.

- Feel the flex of your spirit. Push your awareness out, but this time not into a bubble or shield, but outwards, seeking the land.

- Use your conscious knowledge to begin with, to imagine your way down the road, away from your house, to some distant point, a hill or forest.

- Come back and go in a different direction. Follow the contours of a hill, climb to the top, look at the view.

- Go upwards, high into the sky in an air-balloon, and look down, see your neighbourhood stretched out beneath you.

- Look up at the stars, as you float in your balloon under them. See how vast and wondrous the sky is.

- You can stretch great distances, and if you are quiet enough in doing so, you can feel the land, its life, its many features, its spirit.

- Reach out and bless the land with your love. You are part of its geography, as it is part of you. There is no real separation. Everything has spirit.

EVERYTHING HAS SPIRIT, AND WE MUST COME TO live our lives collectively in the knowledge and acknowledgement of this. Do the exercise above daily, nightly, until your heart is filled with the reality of where you live and what you are a part of. Learn to bless the land – speak your blessings out loud, don't be shy. Give your thanks to all creatures, the spirit of the water you drink, the rain that falls on the trees, the trees themselves, and onwards.

Become part of the world. Not in dominion over it, but as an essential, graceful part of it.

Then go forward and share your love and respect for it all.

AFTERWORD

I think we're done! You've learnt the basics of grounding, centring, shielding, and filtering, which is the perfect introduction to developing your inner world, to soulwork and energy work, to connecting with spirit, to doing magic. You also have some great ideas for developing these methods into daily rituals, and for using them in practical ways in your day to day life.

All you must do now is keep practicing and explore where these exercises might take you. Because I can guarantee it – they'll take you somewhere extraordinary.

My brightest blessings on you!

P.S. If you visit www.katherinegenet.online, you will find a growing collection of resources, books such as this guide, associated audio files, and of course, my novels.

ABOUT THE AUTHOR

Katherine has been walking the Pagan path for thirty years, with her first book published in her home country of New Zealand while in her twenties, on the subject of dreams. She spent several years writing and teaching about dreamwork and working as a psychic before turning to novel-writing, studying creative writing at university while raising her children and facing chronic illness.

Since then, she has published more than twenty long and short novels and writes under various pen names in more than one genre.

Now, her main focus are short guides to magic, and pagan-themed novels containing old and wild truths, for anyone who loves a good story and a world filled with magic.

Katherine lives in the South Island of New Zealand with her wife Valerie. She is a mother and grandmother.

Made in the USA
Middletown, DE
29 June 2023